MILLION DOLLAR PLAYBOOK

How Changing Your Mind Will Make You Millions

By Enzo Fiore

ENZO FIORE
MILLION DOLLAR PLAYBOOK

FOREWORD

My name is Enzo Fiore, and I am a real estate agent and sales coach in Beverly Hills, California. My real estate team and I have over $2 billion in closed real estate transactions. Though I have been in real estate for 4 years now, I have not always been showing $5 million dollar properties and making six figures a year... I grew up in a small town outside of Boston, Massachusetts called Kingston. Growing up, I was never exposed to the different ways people were living. I only saw what was right in front of me, in my town. Until I got my first Ipad and discovered Youtube, I did not know that millions of people throughout the world were making millions of dollars. I thought to myself, why do I have to go to college and get a job, when this won't give me the life that I see these people living? I knew I needed to surround myself with people who were already at that level, or who were on their way there.

When I was 15, my incredible parents made the decision to move to Los Angeles, California so that I could pursue my dreams and goals. They did not just decide to make the move.... I sold them on it. Two years earlier, I made a long powerpoint on the best schools in LA, the plus's of living in the city, why it was the place to be, I even submitted them for jobs through job sites to secure it. Finally, I had presented it. Within two seconds, I heard "no" from both of them. This was a roadblock, but I did not stop there. Whenever I could, I would bring up things about LA, I presented the powerpoint again, and I definitely wasn't accepting "no" for an answer. Finally, after two years of relentless and persistent selling, I had sold them . We packed up, and moved to Los Angeles. When I got to the city, my world changed. I saw Ferrari's, Rolls Royce's, $50m houses. I had arrived to the promised land. This is the moment I realized enormous success was possible for me, and anyone else who was willing to go out and get it. You can escape the 9-5 rat race, and I will show you how - step by step. WARNING! WHAT YOU ARE ABOUT TO READ WILL CHANGE YOUR LIFE.

> **IF YOU AREN'T BUILDING YOUR OWN EMPIRE, YOU ARE BUILDING SOMEONE ELSE'S**
>
> ENZO FIORE

DECIDE. COMMIT. EXECUTE. WIN.

INTRODUCTION

The first step to escaping the normal 9-5 and climbing to greatness is your mindset. If you often find yourself constantly struggling to come up with a plan to change things in your life for the better, you immediately put yourself in a negative state of mind. Planning for hours and weeks for one decision is very detrimental to anyone's mindset. When people are constantly telling you that your ideas are not possible, you can't get it done, wealth is for a select few, or that changing your habits is not necessary for you to succeed, it is important to keep your composure and not to take these criticisms personally. Most people have done the same things consistently for several years, and he or she may be resistant to the change. These people don't know what it takes to get there, and they sure as hell don't know that it's possible. These people are what I call small minded. They are not striving for greatness. They don't want to build an empire. Don't take advice from them. Do not allow yourself to fall into their trap; shake it off and move on. Do not allow other people's negativity to change or force you into a state of resistance; you will become frustrated and will begin to question your own capabilities. Remember, knowing you can change the world and build an empire, and making the commitment to success will continue to feed the world positive energy, and it is that energy that drives improvement and change. **People who are in the mindset of fear of change can stop change.** Continue to learn and improve yourself and your skills to maximize wins and success in your life.

INTRODUCTION PART 2

Results will only happen if you are willing to adapt and change your way of thinking. Once you have mastered this, you will be able to learn so much more about your own capabilities and where to improve. Take learning to walk as an example: as a toddler learning to walk, you probably took several falls but yet got right back up and tackled the challenge. This is a natural reaction for a toddler. First you learn to crawl, then walk, then eventually run. This same concept can be applied to the "adult world." You may be presenting change to someone, and you get knocked down by their limited mindset. Don't allow yourself to stay down: get right back up and start pushing for change again. **That is the mindset you need to be in to maximize your productivity and continuously improve yourself.** Life is a learning process: you will always be learning regardless of how old you are. **Learn how to build an empire.**

EMPIRE STATE OF MIND

Have you ever met someone that has an amazing talent, but instead of capitalizing on it or creating a business out of it, they would rather live a mediocre life, working a boring, unfulfilling 9-5 job? Can you imagine a better ball player than Jordan, a better actress than Kathy Bates, a better motivator than Tony Robbins, a better cook than Paula Dean or a better speaker than Oprah? Of course you can! Talented and gifted people are everywhere! Unfortunately, these are the same people who choose not to share their talents with the world simply because they don't believe in themselves, believe in their talents or believe that they are capable of success. These same beliefs come from social media, the idea of 'overnight success, and popular belief that holds many people back from realizing their true potential and achieving unimaginable, but realistic success. Many of us don't believe that our dreams can come true, so we don't chase them. Instead, we just conform and accept life the way it is. How sad is that? When I was working at Ralph's bagging groceries in 2015, I was surrounded by people who had amazing gifts but did absolutely nothing with them.

Instead, they would rather waste their energy complaining about how unfair life is, and how much they hate their jobs. Is that any kind of way to live? So, if you have ever wondered why success happens to others and not you, realize there are only 2 steps to get there. Change your mind and know, truly know, that you are capable of all of your dreams. **I don't care how big they are. $1,000,000 a year. Completely, unquestionably achievable.** I actually think you should aim higher. The second step is to act on your goals and implement 20x the action (calls, meetings, etc) than you think it takes to get there. **Then, you will start making waves in your life, and you will start achieving.**

If you questioned the $1,000,000 a year being achievable, you may have your mind set on a certain belief.

DECIDE. COMMIT. EXECUTE. WIN.

99% of people have limiting beliefs and or opinions about themselves and their capabilities.

MINDSETS THAT WILL KILL YOUR CHANCE OF SUCCESS

The Limitations Mindset

This is one of the worst mindsets to have. This mindset is like a stop sign. Every time there is an opportunity to grow in some way, you subconsciously stop yourself from moving forward. Have you ever heard someone proclaim, "The sky is the limit?" What a powerful way to think! People with a limitations mindset believe there is a limit to everything; the amount of people they can serve, the amount of money they can make, the level of success they can achieve, etc. They believe that there is a limit to life. These people do not understand that everyone is capable of building an empire. This may be due to what you've been told by parents, teachers, or other people as a child.

The Blamer Mindset

I think we all have come across someone who blames any and everybody for where they are in life. They blame their lack of success on their childhood, a dysfunctional parent, their environment, their friends, etc. The list can go on and on. You see, people with this type of mindset will ALWAYS find something or someone to blame for THEIR actions and where THEY are in their lives. Having this type of mindset will prevent you from holding yourself accountable. If you don't hold yourself accountable, then you can't focus on improving, progressing, growing or moving forward. Have you ever noticed that people with this mindset also seem to go with the flow of things? They don't know what they are doing from one day to the next and always appear uptight. That's because they are stuck in a rut of blaming and not claiming. Claim success today and leave the blames behind. Please repeat after me, "No one has control over my life but me!" Write this down 10 times and read it every morning.

CALL TO ACTION

 IF YOU RELATE TO ANY OF THESE MINDSETS, ASK YOURSELF. WHAT EVENT OR PAST EVENT LED ME TO THINK LIKE THIS? EVALUATE IT, THEN MAKE THE SWITCH.

DECIDE. COMMIT. EXECUTE. WIN.

CHAPTER 2

TAKE ENORMOUS ACTION TO REACH MASSIVE GOALS

TAKING ACTION

Massive actions produce massive results. Taking massive actions is one of the must-take steps if you want to achieve your goals. Once you've set your massive and obsessive goals, then you should take constant, enormous action. Only by doing so, you will get nearer and nearer towards your goals. The moment you take action, there are only two possible outcomes. One is that you have achieved what you wanted, and we call that success. The other outcome is pretty much the opposite, you did not achieved what you wanted. **It is not failure, but feedback.** You will have to change your strategies and plans, and then take massive action again. Know this fact; most people do not achieve what they want the first time. Just like Thomas Edison... he discovered the material for light bulb after 10,000 tries. The same goes if your goal is to reach $10,000,000. You are most likely not going to achieve complete financial freedom in the first few days after you take massive actions, not the first few months, and most likely not the first year. **Take action and sacrifice today, so that you don't have to 10 years down the line.** What you are experiencing today is a result of what actions you've taken in the past. If you are experiencing great results in your life, it is because you've taken massive action in the past. The same goes if you are experiencing mediocre results today... it is because you never really took any actions in the past. Maybe you did take actions, but you gave up. As long as you take massive and constant actions, even if your plan or strategy is off, you will get results.

Most people say that they are going to take action to achieve their goals, but in the end they never actually do anything about it. This is what is happening to most of us; we never really put our words into actions. If you want to become a Millionaire, you can choose to buy a lot of financial and money making books. However, by merely reading these books alone, it won't make you a Millionaire. You will have to apply what you learned, in massive quantities. **If you are reading this book, start taking massive action on all of your goals and dreams, TODAY.** If you do so, you are going to discover that you are moving one step closer to your goal each day.

DECIDE. COMMIT. EXECUTE. WIN.

DECIDE. COMMIT. EXECUTE. WIN.

WHY TAKE MASSIVE ACTION?

You can talk a good game but it's only when you actually step up to the plate and take action that your fears show up. **You must become aware of what's holding you back, otherwise you will never be able to move forward.** Ultimately, there is only one thing that can keep you from your success - **You!** The problem is that your self-limiting beliefs and perceptions are unconscious; meaning you have no idea that you have them. They shall remain nameless, secretly throwing up barriers to your success in the recesses of your mind, until you take action. Then, they pop up and stare you in the face. Now you can examine them for the falsehoods that they are. Mind you, they are always falsehoods and misperceptions, but until you examine them, they remain the boogeyman that's hiding in the dark and scaring the pants off of you. When you find yourself continuously shrinking from certain tasks begin writing down reason you need to be successful. **Who do you do it for? Why do you do it?** Then, write down what you feel before you take action. Write down what comes up, uncensored. Perhaps you'll become aware that you don't want to call anybody because you think the person on the other end of the line won't want to talk to you. Ask yourself, Where did this belief come from? It's quite possible that you'll get a picture of a situation, from way back when you were little. Maybe your big brother shoved you aside and told you to shut up because you were an "annoying little twerp". It was typical big brother stuff, no big deal, but unknowingly you carried it all the way into adulthood and now you're still thinking, deep down, that you're annoying, and that everybody hates you and nobody wants to talk to you. You may have to do the journaling thing over and over again. The original experience formed neural connections in your brain. Your neural connections are like roads along which your thoughts' energy travels. As you are taking action, reframing the old experiences, you are building new neural connections, new roads, along which your thought energy will travel. You'll find that it becomes easier and easier to pick up that phone. Occasionally, the old fear will pop up, as an unconscious thought travels down the wrong road. **Don't freak out; just make it a point to get back on the new road the moment you notice.**

DECIDE. COMMIT. EXECUTE. WIN.

WHY TAKE MASSIVE ACTION?

Finally, the SECOND reason why action is critical. You've faced the dragons; you've reframed your old fears and the thing you never thought would happen, is happening: **You find yourself actually looking forward to picking up the phone!** What??!!! All the positive energy that surrounds you is making things fall into place everywhere, and suddenly you find yourself developing confidence and courage. Nothing breeds confidence like success and nothing solidifies success more than confidence; it's the ultimate Catch 22. **Confidence creates the boldness that is required for greatness.** Remember, what distinguished the influencers wasn't their hard work; it was their courage to boldly follow their sense of purpose and to choose in favor of the things they were passionate about. What made them great is that they let nothing stand in their way. Now, it's time for you to not let anything stand in your way. Do you sense your purpose within? The world is waiting for the contribution that, out of seven billion people, only you can make. Take action and you'll find that you truly are powerful beyond measure.

> "I missed all of the shots I didn't take.
>
> — MICHAEL JORDAN

DECIDE. COMMIT. EXECUTE. WIN.

CHAPTER 3

EVERYTHING IN LIFE IS SELLING

SELLING IS THE ANSWER TO SUCCESS

Robert Louis Stevenson said 'Everything in Life is Selling' and it is. Whether it's a child who cries until they get what they want; whether it's an adult providing a service to their employer in return for payment; or whether it's a guy selling his dream girl on why he's the best man for her, **everything in life is a sale.** Selling is required to reach the upper echelons of wealth and success. If you have millions or billions on your mind, you need to know how to sell. If you want fame and notoriety, you need to know how to sell. *Selling is applicable in every career and situation in life, and if you know how to master it, you will get further than you have ever dreamed of, in every area of your life.* Selling has been with us forever. It could be said that the first salesperson was probably the Serpent in the Garden of Eden. Selling apples in return for infinite wisdom may seem far removed from your own life, but they are nevertheless linked. Selling is a professional skill which can be learned by anyone wanting to learn. Sales skills are not inherent. You can learn the same skills used by the most successful of salespeople but that does not guarantee that you will be successful in sales. As with anything that is skills based, ultimate *success relies on commitment, drive, determination and persistance.*

DECIDE. COMMIT. EXECUTE. WIN.

SELLING IS VITAL

- There is nothing new in selling. Most courses and most theories of selling look remarkably the same, simply because the basics of selling hold true whichever environment you work in.

- Selling is a lot simpler than some people make it out to be. That simplicity however belies the need to work hard at it. Acquiring sales skills requires significant practice.

- Selling is an honourable profession with a dishonourable reputation

- Some people appear to do it naturally

The problem is that while the skills of selling be learned by everybody, not everybody wants to learn the skills. People do not realize the true necessity and importance of selling. It is possible to provide you with all the knowledge and skills you will need to be a successful salesperson, but unless you have the right attitude towards selling, then knowing how to sell won't get you anything. Here are some basic principles about selling and your role in the success of your family, life, etc.

Treat Selling as a Profession
The reason why most people do not regard selling as a profession is that too many salespeople do not treat it as a profession. Professionals embark upon their careers by studying the subject in some depth; become qualified in their profession; practice the skills relentlessly; and update their knowledge and skills regularly.

Accept Personal Responsibility for Sales Success
There is no such thing as luck in selling. Successful salespeople make their own luck. They make sure to be in the right place at the right time with the right product. Your sales success is dependent upon you and no one else. If you know how to sell and how to overcome every possible objection, and you know how to close, than you will undoubtably sell like a machine. Accepting personal responsibility puts you in charge.

Understand Yourself
If you analysed what motivates you, you will be well on the road to knowing what motivates others. Self-analysis is a prerequisite for sales success. Set goals, priorities and deadlines. Those who are achievers do not rely on luck, but have a game plan that they work on. They know what they want, and work towards achieving it. Understand that Customers will buy 'expensive' when appropriate If people only bought what was cheap then all companies would be selling the same thing. There are companies selling items which are more expensive than yours and companies selling items which are cheaper than yours. People buy what they believe satisfies what they want. Your own house is crammed full of things which you could not justify on price alone - your customers are the same. Most customers buy things without comparing, if you are sold that your product is the best out there. Think of the last five items you bought and what comparisons you made before parting with your money.

DECIDE. COMMIT. EXECUTE. WIN.

SELLING IS VITAL

Age, Gender and Experience Count for Nothing
Successful salespeople come in all ages, from each gender, and have varying degrees of experience. Sales success is no respecter of age or experience. Buyers will buy from people whom they trust. Just because someone has 10+ years experience in selling, does not mean they are a professional.

Persevere
Your attitude should be that everyone wants to buy from you. Providing that you keep in touch on a regular basis, one day you will be in the right place at the right time with the right proposal. Most unsuccessful salespeople stop contacting customers just before they buy. Learning is a never-ending experience. Someone once said 'To cease to learn is to cease to live'. I encourage you to live a little.

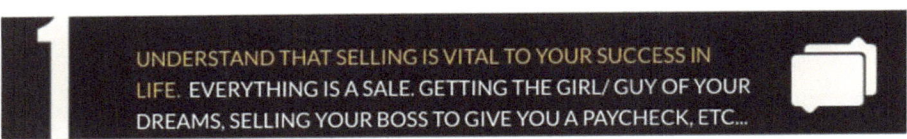

1. UNDERSTAND THAT SELLING IS VITAL TO YOUR SUCCESS IN LIFE. EVERYTHING IS A SALE. GETTING THE GIRL/ GUY OF YOUR DREAMS, SELLING YOUR BOSS TO GIVE YOU A PAYCHECK, ETC...

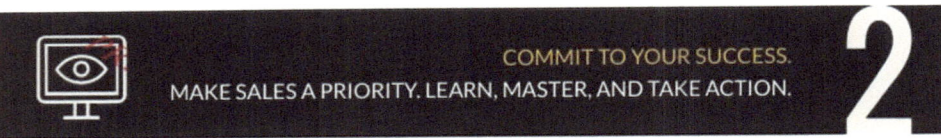

2. COMMIT TO YOUR SUCCESS. MAKE SALES A PRIORITY. LEARN, MASTER, AND TAKE ACTION.

Did you know?

99%

of the population are **not taking enough action.**

DECIDE. COMMIT. EXECUTE. WIN.

CHAPTER 4

BEING SURROUNDED BY SUCCESS AND GETTING THE WORLD TO KNOW YOU

OMNIPRESENCE

When I first moved to Los Angeles, I can't tell you how many times I heard people say "I know Justin Bieber's sisters friend" or "I know Brad Pitt", or something similar to this. I would always think to myself, yes these people "know" all of these celebrities, but do these celebrities know them?

The answer is 99% NO.

Chances are, you've heard the quote "It's all about who you know." This quote sounds nice, but what if these people that you know don't know you. They are not such a useful network anymore. Instead of who you know, you need to focus on WHO KNOWS YOU! When you start to make this your mission, you can start upping your goals. Once you get 10k people to know you through social media, you move it up to 100.

Here are 2 key focuses for your social media, and ways you can get you or your company in front of the world.

GET DISCOVERED:

If you don't have every social media network branded with your business, this is a must. Keep it consistent throughout every profile. If you post once or twice a day, you are thinking WAY too small. If you think one or two posts are going to get you noticed, you have underestimated the size of the internet and the amount of profiles and people out there. Your biggest problem is obscurity—other people aren't thinking about you. POST 10X MORE.

BREAK THROUGH THE NUMBERS:

You have to get creative to break through all of the noise that is social media. There are 7+ billion people in the world, and most of them are on social media. Don't be careful with posts, and don't be afraid to be offensive or afraid to make a mistake. The biggest mistake you will make is not getting known by the world. It will cost you MILLIONS, if not BILLIONS of dollars.

DECIDE. COMMIT. EXECUTE. WIN.

YOUR CIRCLE

Always pay attention to who you let into your circle and life .
Negative people will always find a way to complain, bad things always happen to them, and they are always jealous of other people.

If you want wealth and success, you can't be afraid of cutting people out of your life.

You need to be around smarter, more successful, and like minded people.

This is more important than you think.

The people that you spend the most time with affect your mood, goals, vision for the future, and if you aren't careful, they can diminish your success and forward progress.

You need to start cutting people out. Lots of people may be offended by this, but this is a game changer for your success.

If all your friends want to do is smoke weed, party, and play video games…. and you want to build an empire and make $10 million, these probably aren't the people you should be surrounding yourself with.

Surround yourself with people who are winning, working at their goals, who have a huge vision for their future. It will change your life.

Once I took control of my friends, my success and finances went through the roof.
You need to be more picky…….

DECIDE. COMMIT. EXECUTE. WIN.

THINK DIFFERENTLY

IF YOU WANT WEALTH AND SUCCESS, YOU NEED TO THINK ABOUT MONEY DIFFERENTLY.

I want to show you how wealthy people get wealthier, and poor people stay poor. As I was growing up, I was always told: money doesn't grow on trees, $100,000 is a lot of money, don't waste your money, save it, buy a house etc. When I started really committing to my success and growth, I started learning that all the things I learned growing up about money were totally wrong. Let's look at how wealthy people spend money, and how poor people spend money.

Wealthy

Invest in their education, development, and personal motivation
Willingly trade money for knowledge, attention, network.
Spend money to invest.
Expand their network.
Multiply income with multiple flows.
Take responsibility for everything that happens
Abundance Mentality.

Average

Spend on clothing, cars, video games, and products that don't create more money.
Save money
Time wasting habits- watching TV, scrolling instagram, video games
One source of income
Point fingers when bad things happen, always complaining.
Scarcity mentality- They think that they cannot create wealth

Look, the difference between the wealthy and the average is the way that money is used. Average people use money to spend on entertainment, clothing, gambling, and more products that won't return on their investment. Wealthy people only spend on things that will make them money. They use money as a tool rather than wasting it. Start spending like the wealthy. It will change the game for you.
The most important takeaway from this is to

1. CREATE CASH FLOW.
2. DON'T RELY ON ONE SOURCE OF INCOME.

YOU WILL NEVER CREATE WEALTH FROM JUST ONE SOURCE OR FLOW.

DECIDE. COMMIT. EXECUTE. WIN.

GET STARTED

Would you like to see more success in your life?
Would you like your life to be filled with **more abundance, money, success, and more?**
If you've answered "yes" to any of these questions, **then it is clear that you need to take some action to change your life, to become more successful.**
Your life won't change one day when you wake up - you're going to have to be the change.

The first thing that you must understand is that your life is not the product or even by-product of outside events. World economic conditions, local market forces, tax rates, the boss who bullies you, the work you don't like - all these external events have nothing to do with your success or failure - they only play the role of catalyst in the life that you, yourself, have fashioned for yourself.

All these externalities are only minor ingredients in the "cake of life" - you're the one who bakes it - it can either flop in the middle or you can be a master chef.   The choice is yours as to how you work with the conditions in which you find yourself - whether that's a horrible job, poor economic conditions, a failing personal relationship or a really good job, but one that takes up all of your time and energy to the detriment of your personal life.

First of all, if you don't like your work, it has nothing to do with the work, it has everything to do with your mindset. If you find yourself in troubled economic or competitive conditions, then let those conditions be the stimulus for you to take real action. Don't follow the herd. It amazes me the number of times that I have recently been told by business people facing falling sales that they were cutting their marketing efforts - presumably with the objective of making their sales fall further!!

Be different - take action.

DECIDE. COMMIT. EXECUTE. WIN.

GET STARTED

Don't react the way normal people do -
anytime we react, we make matters worse.
And therein lies the key to being the change that you want to see in your life.
The normal person constantly and automatically reacts to what is going on around them, believing themselves to be the victim of circumstance.
No - they are the victim of their own minds, minds that are running on autopilot, that is looking out the back window and never actually sees what's really happening as it happens!

Don't be focused on the past. Create your future. If you answered "yes" to the questions at the start of this article, you need to take real action - and stop the automatic reaction. The first thing you need to do is decide what you want out of life. Wow - that's a big question - "what do I want out of life?" - but, until you have some idea of what you want and why you're doing what you're doing, then it makes sense that you still haven't found what you're looking for!! You need to define what success and happiness means for you - what it would look like, feel like, sound like, smell like, taste like - You then need to start acting rather than reacting.

Our normal behaviour is reactionary - we are, in effect, creatures of habit, performing all our routine tasks using that backward-looking autopilot. And, if you reflect on it for a moment, pretty much everything we do in life becomes routine, sooner or later. You've got to switch the autopilot off.

This sets you up for a different life - it enables you become attentive to your state of mind, attentive to whether you're acting or reacting. This attentiveness is all you need to begin to do more important things differently - it enables you act, rather than react. As sure as night follows day, your automatic behaviours will give way to real action - and you'll experience the difference in your life, when it matters.

Believe me, some people, who have only seen me speak for ten minutes, but who have then put this into practice email me, telling me that it has changed their lives. You see, to change your life you simply need to change your mind - because, as things stand, your mind creates your life automatically.

Take charge of your control systems, chart your course for the kind of success and happiness that turns you on and, then, little by little, step by step, action by action, that life you really want will simply emerge.

IF YOU AREN'T BUILDING YOUR EMPIRE, YOU ARE BUILDING SOMEONE ELSE'S.

DECIDE. COMMIT. EXECUTE. WIN.

ENZO ENTERPRISES

GOAL SETTING AND EXECUTION PHONE SESSION

PLAN YOUR GOALS, AND GET CUSTOM ACTION PLAN TO NAIL EACH GOAL

WWW.THEENZOFIORE.COM/SCHEDULE

Enzo Fiore

DECIDE. COMMIT. EXECUTE. WIN.

www.ingramcontent.com/pod-product-compliance
Lightning Source LLC
Chambersburg PA
CBHW041319180526
45172CB00004B/1155